This is the true story of a br
lived nearly two thousand y

Boudicca was a tall woman with long red hair.
She wore a cloak and dress of many colours.
Her people were called the Iceni.
She was their queen.

People called the Romans came from
across the sea.
The Iceni tried to make friends with them.

But the Romans stole their money and took away their farms.

Boudicca loved her land and her people.
She tried to stop the Romans.
The Romans whipped Boudicca and her
daughters.

Boudicca was very angry!
"We will fight the Romans," she said.
"We will burn Colchester!"

Colchester was a town the Romans
had built.
Many people lived there.
There were houses, shops and a temple.

Boudicca's army set fire to Colchester.
They killed the people and stole everything.
"On to London!" said Boudicca.
"We will burn all the Roman towns!"

The Romans were very afraid.
The leader of the Roman army was
called Suetonius.
"We must stop this queen," he said.

The Roman army met Boudicca's army.
Boudicca's army was much bigger.
Boudicca was sure she would win.

She told all the women and children to put
their wagons in a long line behind her army.
She wanted the women and children to
watch her army win.

Boudicca rode in her chariot all around her army.
"Be strong and brave!" she said.
"We are like wolves, but the Romans are like rabbits!"

Suetonius spoke to his army.
"Do not be afraid of this woman," he told them.
"There are only a few of us, but
we are the best fighters in the world."

There was a terrible battle.
Boudicca's army was brave, but
the Romans were stronger.

Boudicca's men tried to escape.
But the wagons were in the way.
They were trapped!
The Romans killed men, women and children.

"I cannot stop the Romans," said Boudicca.
"But I will not let them catch me."
And so brave Queen Boudicca drank
some poison and died.